Desipreneur 0.0

How To Think Before You Start

Santhosh Muruganantham

INDIA • SINGAPORE • MALAYSIA

Notion Press

No.8, 3rd Cross Street
CIT Colony, Mylapore
Chennai, Tamil Nadu – 600004

First Published by Notion Press 2021
Copyright © Santhosh Muruganantham 2021
All Rights Reserved.

ISBN 978-1-63781-510-6

This book has been published with all efforts taken to make the material error-free after the consent of the author. However, the author and the publisher do not assume and hereby disclaim any liability to any party for any loss, damage, or disruption caused by errors or omissions, whether such errors or omissions result from negligence, accident, or any other cause.

While every effort has been made to avoid any mistake or omission, this publication is being sold on the condition and understanding that neither the author nor the publishers or printers would be liable in any manner to any person by reason of any mistake or omission in this publication or for any action taken or omitted to be taken or advice rendered or accepted on the basis of this work. For any defect in printing or binding the publishers will be liable only to replace the defective copy by another copy of this work then available.

Contents

Acknowledgement		5
Epigraph		7
Preface		9
1.	It's Not All About the Looks!	15
2.	Reputation Starts Yesterday	23
3.	The Three Wheels of Your Auto	33
4.	Employment Upside Down	41
5.	Ice Cube Effect	47
6.	Risky is the New Sexy	53
7.	Predict or Perish	59
8.	Profit vs The Learning Curve	65
9.	The Anticlimax	69
10.	Just Jump!	77
11.	The Indian Edge	83
12.	Cardinal Rules	95

Acknowledgement

There are a lot of people who I want to thank and yes, I'm ever grateful to you who have bought this book and invested in me. So, thank you, my reader.

It has been a rollercoaster ride for me and I would like to thank the people who have kept rooting for me and our business, definitely a special mention to my parents, Mr Muruganantham and Mrs Adilakshmi for allowing me to become myself, to my ultra-amazing wife Sanchitha who actually asked me to chase my dreams when I was about to send out my resume to companies, to my sister Sunitha who has been blindly supportive and also a shoutout to my in-laws Mr. Suresh and Mrs. Vasumathi for being the real cheerleaders.

I need to thank my partners Adithya Raju, Padmanabhan (childhood friend from Grade 3) and Senthil Kumar. My uncle Ramanathan who was the first to invest in us and my schoolmate Syed Sarfaz, who not only invested but also sowed the seed to evangelize Kolapasi.

To my mentors Joy Mediratta and Rajesh Srivastava who have nurtured and guided me to become the person I am today.

Finally, a big hug to the entire Kolapasi family (employees and customers) for building the brand and giving us an identity, if it's not for you guys showing all the love, we wouldn't be an international brand today.

I am immensely grateful to the people who made this book what it is today, Sneha Rao for helping me to write this book, Priyadarshini for illustrating this book and Sanjana Uppili who is responsible for helping me in publishing this book through Notion Press.

Epigraph

Running a business is like running a marathon, it's not a sprint. You cannot decide that you want to run a marathon today and run one tomorrow. If you do, you are more likely to faint after the 4th or 5th mile. You need to build stamina, practice regularly and train hard, watch your diet and get enough sleep. Similarly, you must be mentally prepared and understand what it takes to run a business. This book is an attempt to tune you into an entrepreneurial mindset and get some basics right.

Preface

Who Is This Book For?

I assume the reason you picked this book is because you are bit by the bug, "One day, I will start my own business" – the Entrepreneurship bug. Well! Welcome to the club. I was bit by the bug too, a long while ago – pretty much during my college days.

Close to 80% of the people I meet resonate with the same thought. They are bustling with ideas and are mere inches away from starting their own venture. Yet they struggle to make the leap, held back by the fear of uncertainty, confused by questions like – "If only I knew which idea I should work on?" or "How do I convince my family?" and most often, "When is the right time to start my business and more importantly, how do I raise the money?"

This book is for those of you who have burning questions like these in your mind. Desipreneur 0.0 is targeted towards guiding you through the thought process on how to think before you start your business, to bridge between your uncertainties and give wings to your venture. I respect your money more than my money and by saying so, if, after reading this book, you think it has not added value to the price you paid, I will be the happiest person to refund your money. You have trusted me and accepted to trade your hard-earned money to buy this book and all I aim to do is nothing but to do justice to your trust. Hit me up at instagram.com/santhosh_muruganantham for your refund if necessary.

Why Did I Write This Book?

So, you might now be thinking about why I wrote this book. When I wanted to read about how to start a business, there was no dearth of books. But strangely enough, all of them were about huge successful multi-billion-dollar businesses. I know that I would not be Apple or Google (not at the very beginning at least). These books were pretty high brow for me (I felt kind of like a kindergarten student reading Engineering textbooks). I wanted a book that taught me how to get to the Second Grade. I wanted a book that told a novice like me how to think like an entrepreneur and start my own business. A book for a first-time entrepreneur who wanted to go from wanting to become an entrepreneur to becoming one. But I found that there was very little in that category around 2010-2013. That, in a nutshell, is why I wanted to write this book, so people who are beginners like me can easily connect to a small-time entrepreneur than vis a vis to a full-blown established entrepreneur.

Preface

This book is about the reflection of the few things we did right and more of what we did wrong before we started. It dwells on how these thought processes shaped the future of our venture. Basically, it is the foundation on top of which our enterprise was built on. This is not all that it takes. In this book, I'm only covering the thought processes one needs to start an enterprise. The next book will cover more on what you need to do after you start.

During my 10 years of full-time Entrepreneurship, I have seen an enormous number of entrepreneurs who started their venture on their wrong foot. The foundation was still not strong enough for them to scale. It made me wish that I had an opportunity to share what I learnt from my mistakes with them before they started the venture. I would have gladly passed on this book to them. It could have saved months, if not years of their toil. As we all know, if the foundation is not right, it's almost impossible to build a growing scalable business. The business might run, but the chances to scale it to the next level is very less.

My Exciting Journey So Far In A Nutshell!

Now, I anticipate you might ask this question – Do I have the credentials to talk about this topic?

That is the perfect question to ask.

Preface

Maybe, I might have a little bit of knowledge to share (given the years of hard work with mistakes and some reasonably good decisions thrown in).

Let me take the time to introduce myself. I come from a simple, middle-class Indian background with zero business acumen passed on to me from my parents or family. My mom worked for BSNL (central government) and my father was a state kabaddi coach (worked for the Sports Development Authority of Tamil Nadu). My elder sister is an ex-National volleyball player and is now an officer with Southern Railways. I studied at SBOA School, Anna Nagar (Chennai) and did my B. Tech (IT) from Sriram Engineering College (Veppampattu). I did my Masters in Bioinformatics at Georgia Institute of Technology (Atlanta) and worked in the USA for about 6 years. Then, I came back to India to start an enterprise. About 8 years ago, we (my friends Adithya Raju and Padmanabhan) started Kolapasi and later Senthil Kumar joined us. Today, it's a takeaway restaurant chain with multiple outlets across South India. We are also expanding internationally with the upcoming launch in Melbourne, Australia by 2021 and considering proposals to launch in the UK, USA, Malaysia, Singapore through franchising in a year or two.

Preface

Before Kolapasi, I partnered with a friend to start a retail garment showroom in Hyderabad and was into the Import & Export of garments. I have also traded stocks and options during my stint in the US.

It's Not All About the Looks!

"Don't fall in love with your neighbour just because the person looks stunning"

You are probably looking at the title of the chapter and wondering, "What's that got to do with me starting a business?"

Let me explain. Time travel, back to your teens. You had a group of friends and knew a lot of people, went to school and had loads of fun? Who was your first crush? The hottest boy or girl you knew? Because you thought that person is so attractive you would impress other people around you or maybe even make them jealous?

But now, when you look back, would they have been the right one for you? In most cases, the answer would probably be a no.

This pretty much applies to your business too. You might see or know someone who is a successful entrepreneur. They are doing so well and are having a very fancy life. So, you think, "Hey! That's a great idea! Let me do that." But no. What might work for that person, may not work for you. And what might not work for someone might work for you. One man's trash is another man's treasure, right?! So, before you jump the gun and leap on the entrepreneur bandwagon, think deep and hard on reasons why you are doing it and if it is the best business for you.

Let me share my experience with you. In 2010, I had returned to India, after spending eight years in the United States of America. Upon returning, my urge to become an entrepreneur resurfaced. I had this idea – to make real American branded clothing available in India. I thought it was a brilliant idea. Of course, when you have such a great idea, you want to tell your people about it, right? But guess what, when I told people about this idea, they thought I had gone crazy.

But what I knew personally, was that almost every household in Hyderabad had a family member living in the US so, when they came to India for vacations, they would invariably get American branded clothing as gifts and souvenirs from the US. So, many of the households were familiar with American clothing brands and had been getting used to the style, fit and comfort of such brands. So, I thought to myself, "Hey, it looks like Hyderabad is a great market for these American brands!" – for I knew from my personal experience that once people got used to wearing these brands, they would fall in love with them. So, there was this sizeable population who were aware of these brands and probably love them too.

I reasoned with my folks, but they did not take me seriously and they said, "Buying clothes in US dollars?! Selling it in Indian rupees in Hyderabad?! Are you mad?" They did have a valid point from their perspective. Some said, "Most of these clothes are manufactured in Tirupur, India and exported to the US. So, why would anyone want to buy the same thing at such a higher price?" I did not lose heart though. I laughed along with them – but did not give up on the idea.

So, I started to work on my idea. I was completely convinced that it was going to be a good business and I knew it was going to work. So, that's how I started a branded clothing outlet in Hyderabad, where we bought branded clothing from the US and sold it there. Some people were sure that the business would be a flop. But, it didn't. We had customers who were ready to buy a basic round neck tee for INR 2000.

But, would that have worked out in Chennai? Most probably not! Just because I am from Chennai and the city is easy for me and looks good to start a business, I did not settle for it here. I chased the market in Hyderabad because that was right, and I saw potential in it. So similarly, you don't have to start a tech startup just because you have a laptop at your disposal.

So how do you know which idea will work? How to recognize the spark, i.e., the business idea? Well, the idea is like a ghost – it will possess you. If you have it, you will know it. It's like, if you are unable to decide and have to ask someone whether a particular person is the right one for you, then in all probability, that person is not for you. You already have your doubts if it will work out for the good! Similarly, if you have to ask someone if your idea is good, then that is not for you as it shows that you aren't confident about it.

The moment you know that your idea is good, you are thoroughly convinced, and you don't have to ask anyone, that is your ghost – that is your idea, that's what is going to be your journey.

There are many people out there, who think, "I want to start a business, but I don't have an idea." If you don't have an idea, don't start a business. My serious advice for you is – Wait for the idea to possess you. It's just like getting married because all your friends are getting married. Don't do a business, because your friend, relative, colleague, or someone else is doing a business. In fact, instead of looking for an idea, start looking for a problem, preferably your own problem and try to find the best fit solution to it. It is more likely than not that this solution you found could be a great business Idea. For instance, take Resonate, they came up with the idea of a portable pocket-size UPS for your router so that your internet connection does not stop in case of a power cut. It went on to be a huge hit. They found a problem and found an incredibly awesome solution to it!

Your business is like the love of your life. You will do anything for your love, to impress and make them yours. That's how your business idea would make you feel. You will not mind working long hours or going that extra mile when it is your idea.

So, now go find your love... err... I mean... your idea.

Reputation Starts Yesterday

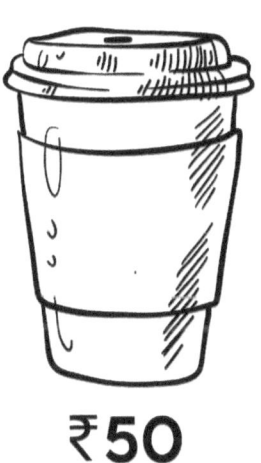 

₹50 ₹150

Most of us tend to fall into the mentality of a rebel entrepreneur. Why? Because we read stories about someone who ran away from their homes to pursue their dreams when none of their friends or family supported them, slept on park benches and platforms, took up all sorts of menial jobs and against all odds they struggled their way up to glory. As much as I admire the hard work and courage of such people, this is the hardest way to become an entrepreneur.

We also want to think that others will fail to understand us and also our bias makes us think we are right, and the world is always wrong. So instead of taking the time to make our close circle understand which is a tougher job, we tend to take the easy route – to become a rebel and blame it on others.

Let me put it this way. You, all of a sudden go and tell your parents that you want to run a business and you ask for money, what do you expect? Of course, they will say no. You have not done anything so far to prove that you are responsible enough to handle that kind of money. It doesn't matter if you are a teen or in your 30's. Unless you have done something to make them realize that you truly are passionate, how can you expect them to be supportive of you while you are yourself alone, haven't proven anything yet and are struggling both mentally and emotionally?

That's the point where many people fail and shut shop and call it quits. Let's say you are one among a million and you manage to face it all alone, but you have no one to celebrate your success story with. Also, business is mainly about people, so you go to your parents to invest in your business, they say no, and you immediately alienate yourself from them. You go to your friends to ask them to be co-founders and they say no, you alienate them too. You somehow manage to start some business, you are trying to scale your business, you need more money, people and all kinds of resources to feed its growth but you need to find skills on how you sell your product/service to your customers. If you are not able to get your people, your parents, your friends and your relatives to believe in you and invest in your idea, it's highly unlikely that you would be able to find customers and other stakeholders to sell and support your product or service. Yes, there are always a few exceptions. But, instead of becoming a rebel, consider your first challenge. In winning this challenge you get to learn how to influence and persuade people and, also you get a bonus point of having your close circle be supportive of your dream. The last thing you want is to handle pressure from your business and pressure at home.

So, now let's get into how to win the hearts of people in your close circle.

Mental Conditioning Programming (MCP)

MCP is a persuasive strategy to make people ease into the idea you want them to buy. You slowly convince your people to get on board and support you, your passion and your ideas. You destroy all the fears and inhibitions they have about your idea and make them logically conclude that your idea is the best. It's like the movie Inception. You plant an idea in the mind, and you watch it grow. Not getting the point? Let me make this idea more relatable to you.

All of you are of age, you should be having a boyfriend/ girlfriend (at least a crush) or should have crossed that age and so you can relate to this.

Let's assume you are in your 20's and how would your parents react if you, all of sudden went and told them that you like someone? Of course, they might be sceptical, might overreact or downright hate the guts of that special someone. They are your parents and they have loved you all their life. Of course, their paternal instincts kick in and they want to protect you. But, you could also follow an alternate approach. Introduce your significant other as a friend, invite them along for a special occasion and get them to meet your parents. Tell your mom how they are a fan of her signature dish, plant a good opinion about them in each other's minds, and let them develop a great opinion of each other. This way, your family might be more receptive and accept it with an open heart when you finally break the news.

Let me share my story of how I convinced my wife's and my own family to accept our relationship. They are vegetarians and we practically eat anything that moves. In all odds, you would be thinking we ran away and eloped. But no, our families were as happy as we were for us to get married. My mom and my mom-in-law became best friends and how did that happen?

When I was working in Atlanta, she also took up a PG program to pursue there. That was in 2007. In 2008 her mother, aunt and a few of her cousins planned a trip to the US, but their first stop was Florida and they were planning to come to Atlanta after a couple of days. But like any sentimental-Indian-loving mother, after missing her daughter for more than a year, she was feeling bad that she had to wait for a few more days to see her daughter despite being in the US. When I heard this from Sanchitha, I seized this opportunity to impress my potential future in-laws. I took her all the way to Florida – an almost 8-hour drive, to meet her parents and relatives. Her mother was super impressed by the gesture. We stayed there for a couple of days and I drove them down to Atlanta and was a perfect host taking them to movies, malls and all sorts of touristy places in and around

Atlanta. During the trip, Sanchitha's aunt told me that they were planning to get her married the next year and I have to find time to visit India to attend her wedding without fail. And I slyly yet politely told her that I will make it and there is no way that she would get married without me being at the wedding. Later that day the cousins heard Sanchitha's mother and her aunt discussing how lucky they would become if they managed to find a groom like me. Obviously, the news got leaked to us by her cousins and Sanchitha made her move and told her mother and aunt that we are fond of each other. Since her mom already was impressed with me, this was not a big shock to her. Now, she took the onus to talk to Sanchitha's dad and assured him that I would be a great fit for their family.

On the other side, I also got my mom and my mom-in-law to like each other by telling them how they admire each other even before they met. I set it up so well for each other that when both the moms met, they had no other choice but to instantly take to each other. From there it was not very difficult to convince our parents to look past caste and creed and get us married. In their eyes, we were a match made in heaven!

Till today both the moms think that it all happened in a fluke, but to their surprise, every single move was planned meticulously.

You have to understand that you are the director of your movie, if you don't direct your movie then the story can take its own twists and turns and most probably the story could turn sour.

So, don't just be the actor in your movie, also make sure you direct it well.

Similarly, before I started Kolapasi, when it was still in the ideation stage, I used to tell my mother about how tasty, yet healthy her biryani is. Praised her cooking skills and got her hooked on the idea. When we wanted to start our kitchen not only did she willingly invest but also supported me in cooking in the kitchen in the initial, crucial months. My wife also was a part of it, she took a loan and invested in the business. All this was possible because they believed in me. More than anything else they believed in the idea. I slowly sold the idea to them and got them on board. Even when I was under pressure and struggling, my parents and my wife stood by me and pushed me to find a way to see through the obstacle and make Kolapasi a reality. Kolapasi, from being my dream, became a collective dream. It became a part of the family and it was fed and nurtured at every stage!

So, now coming back to you, what can you do to win your parents heart? Well, you start with obliging to their picture of an ideal son or daughter. If they want you to study well and get 95% in your exams, do so. If they want you home by 6 pm, be there. If they want you to not spend time playing PubG or mindlessly spending time scrolling through your social media accounts, stop it. Start speaking about your interest in running your own business to your parents. Get them involved before you ask them to invest. Openly discuss whatever information you can share in a manner they will understand. Yes, there is a generation gap, yes, they might not be able to understand all that you say, but they will learn to trust you. Take part in startup seminars, read about the relevant field you want to do business in, start showing your parents that you are really up to something. Then try to convince them to invest. They probably have saved some money to spend on your masters or MBA or your big fat Indian wedding. Tell them you don't want a lavish wedding, or you don't want to pursue higher graduation, instead of gaining more theoretical knowledge, you did rather gain practical knowledge by running your own business. Tell them to invest say Rs 1 lakh for starters, that you will try your hand at your business for a year or so, learn your trade and do everything it takes to be successful. Tell them despite the outcome you would have the satisfaction of giving your dream a fair chance. They will believe in you then. They will happily support you and your dreams. They have the capacity to support your business. And they will do so when they truly trust you.

So, go on and win their hearts!

MCP is a very powerful tool, but make sure you use it for the right reasons. MCP is not taking advantage of people. It's a process of understanding the other person from their perspective and positively influencing them.

Yes, few people might use it with a negative connotation.

It's like a knife. A knife in the hands of a doctor can save lives whereas in the hands of a criminal will take lives.

The Three Wheels of Your Auto

We have all seen an auto. Maybe the first thought, when I mention an auto, is how we all bargain about the fare but let's skip that and think about its wheels instead. You need all the 3 wheels working for you to move ahead and even if one wheel is off then the auto will not move forward and will be running in circles. So, we all agree on how important the wheels are. Now let's think about the basic human necessities – Food, Clothing, Shelter. We all need at least these three things to support our existence. Similarly, every business has some basic necessities – Finance, domain knowledge and Emotional strength. If these needs are not met, you will find the wheels coming off your wagon very soon. Let me explain each of these aspects in more detail.

The Wheel of Finance

There are two main aspects of Finance. One is your personal finance and the other is the Finance needed to run your business. Let's say, you have a well-paying job, you are getting used to a certain lifestyle and those regular vacations. Now you have worked for a couple of years and have a car loan and a home loan. Although you are financially independent, you have so many financial commitments that you cannot quit your job and follow your passion. You have debts and EMIs to pay off and credit card bills to settle, and you are tied down. You raised the stake so high, now you think you can't risk having a dream anymore. After I quit my job, came back to India and started my business, I was clear about one thing – keeping my needs minimal. It has been close to 10 years since I became an entrepreneur. I don't own a car, not because I cannot afford one and I stay in a rented apartment. I have always considered a car to be a depreciating asset, the moment you buy it, it starts depreciating in its value. After coming back to India, I had the money to buy a car, but I chose to invest the money in Kolapasi instead. It made more sense to invest the surplus I had into our business. I realized the importance of keeping my personal needs to the bare minimum so that I could fund and concentrate on my business during its growing years. If you can cover for your personal finance needs and the business needs for say, a period of 6 months to a year, then you can comfortably hang in until you break even, and your business starts picking up!

The Wheel of Knowledge

Product expertise is your knowledge about your offering and your consumer. It's more of a bottoms-up approach. You have to know your audience, their wants, their preferences for your product, to be a hit. That is why many people find great success by finding a solution to their own burning problem because they understand the problem well. It often turns into a brilliant business idea. Let us take Inshorts, the popular news app for example. They found the problem; nobody has the time to read through the long articles in a newspaper to update themselves about the current affairs. They came up with an app that cuts the clutter and delivers the latest news in 60 words. It was a huge hit and moved on to become India's highly rated news app with more than 10 million active users. Though it's a free app for end-users they monetized through advertisements and their annual revenue is now close to Rs 25 crores. They took a problem, found a simple solution, took it to their customers and built a brilliant business around it. Now, do you see why it pays off to know your product and your customers? Focus on your learning curve. Start visualizing the efforts you are going to take. Study the market. Study your target customers. Try to find likeminded people aka your co-founders. You can't build your business alone. You need responsible, driven, enthusiastic likeminded people. Develop the required skill sets – product/service skills and people skills.

The Wheel of Emotion

Emotional intelligence is not just an ability to understand and manage people around you, but also your own self. I do like to think of it as mental conditioning, meaning, developing the grit required to go on till you finish your treasure hunt. Like it is important to learn to handle and associate with people for growing a harmonious business, you also need to learn to handle yourself. Running a business involves a lot of uncertainties. You have to show the ability to learn quickly and take smart timely decisions. And there is no one who has never failed in his life. Business is not an exception. But making a failure your business's tombstone or making it a steppingstone is up to you. You have to have the courage to look past your failures, make them right and grow your business. You will have to learn to stir your ship through the temporary tempests, instead of sinking and hitting rock bottom.

"If you want to be a doer – a person whose life is filled with meaningful experiences, diverse opportunities, and continual learning and growth – then it is essential that you not deplete your confidence and energy by overthinking your opportunities". It's a quote from the famous book, Fail Fast, Fail Often by Ryan Babineaux. You have to learn to grow from your experiences and failures. You have to keep at your goals to finally succeed. The only way to succeed is by not quitting. This is a quality that drives you from the inside when the odds are against you and keeps you focused on the reasons why your business is going to succeed instead of fearing situations where your business fails. Businesses don't fail because of lack of opportunities, but because you are so clouded by the fear of failing that you refuse to see that one opportunity that will launch you to success. You have to keep yourself together and keep your eyes open to seize the opportunity and leap across the chasm of failure. This grit you show will make you realize the burning desire you had when you started your business.

So, are you ready to fuel your tanks yet?

Employment Upside Down

I meet a lot of people who come up to me and say that they are sick and tired of their job and so, they want to become an Entrepreneur. The reason why most of us are not so excited about our jobs is because we see them as one dimensional.

So, let's look at the traditional dictionary definition of Employment

Employment – a noun, the fact of someone being paid to work for a company or organization.

Even you can simplify it by saying that one is trading time for dollars or rupees. So, when we only look at earning money through employment, the job becomes boring and unexciting.

What if we redefine the word Employment for future Entrepreneurs?

Employment – an act where someone is paying you to become an entrepreneur in the future.

Let's assume you want to start a software company. Just imagine all the effort, knowledge and capital needed for you to set up. For one to put all this together it's going to be a herculean task and you will still not know how to go about it after starting one.

Whereas, now imagine yourself getting employed in a software company. Someone else has taken all the risk to put up the framework and system to build a company.

Now the employer thinks that he is paying you for your time. However, you can take it as your learning ground to figure out how to start and run a software company in the future. Now the entire equation changes, you don't have to wait for Fridays to come or get upset on Monday mornings. You are excited every single day, you go to work because your intention is not just to work, but to learn how to start a company in the future. Just a small switch in the way you see employment can have a huge impact on your entrepreneurial journey. Whichever vertical you are looking to start your enterprise, you can go work a couple of years in that vertical to understand the ecosystem.

We tend to separate employment and entrepreneurship however I am saying that they are 2 sides of the same coin.

If you take a step back and look at the bigger picture, an entrepreneur's job is to create a business and to run the business. He/she needs to employ people to execute the jobs since one man cannot run the entire show. So, entrepreneurs pave the way for employment and without an entrepreneur, there's no enterprise for employees to work in.

An entrepreneur exists to create employment. So, one doesn't have to compare Employment and Entrepreneurship. One isn't lesser than the other. In fact, one cannot exist without the other.

Employment is the perfect Gateway to Entrepreneurship. It gives you ample amount of time to size up what you want to do and how you want to do it. You wouldn't know everything on how to start an Enterprise, but enough to build your confidence up to start your new enterprise.

Here are a few things that make employment extremely important!

1. It's a win-win situation where you get to learn and the business that hires you gets work done from you.

2. It's a place which teaches us to understand people and work as a team

3. You get to focus on the job that's assigned to you without worrying about the other aspects of the business. The degree of multitasking involved is a key distinguishing factor that sets entrepreneurship and employment apart.

4. You might also get to switch roles and learn more aspects of the business on a piecemeal basis. If you play it smart you could be learning A to Z about everything that is required to run a business as an employee.

5. You get paid irrespective of the performance of the business. Unless the economy is crumbling, and the business is downsizing/cost-cutting.

6. There is someone to cover up for when you take time off from work. But there is no alternate boss to take over running a business!

I can go on and on about why employment is going to serve as your stepping-stone and provide you with most of the experience you need to run your own show! If you have excellent work ethics and the smarts to pick up the trade, you will make a better entrepreneur after a stint being an employee than if you have to start afresh with zero experience whatsoever. You would notice that the job descriptions today read, candidates with an entrepreneurial spirit are preferred. This is what it means to have an entrepreneurial spirit. Treat employment as your own business. There is a common saying – dress for the job you want and not for the job you have. Similarly, work for where you want to be and not what you have. Stop dropping in late and leaving early from work unnecessarily. Show some interest and conviction and the learning and experience that you gain will definitely pay off

Ice Cube Effect

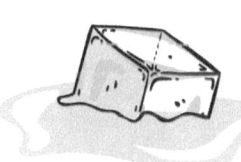

"When you meet people, think you are in a grocery store and pick only what you want to learn and leave. Never complain of what they don't have!"

Have you ever noticed how quickly an ice cube melts on a red-hot summer day? But if you put the same ice cube in the middle of a lot of ice cubes it takes way longer to melt. That is the importance of being in the company of people with the right mindset. If people around you are positive and encouraging, the chances of you being at peace and being patient with your venture is more. Even if you hit a rough patch in your business, they will push to explore new opportunities, innovate and find solutions and move ahead of the challenges you face. They will serve as a source of your strength. Whereas, if the people around you are pessimistic, they are going to suck out all your energy, drag you down and drown you in their misery.

Think about it. We all have those annoying relatives who always want to know how good your scores in an exam are, if you won that tournament, if you got into that prestigious college or if you got the best pay package. They sound like they want the best for you but no matter how well you perform, they say "Oh! my son scored more than that" or "My neighbour's daughter got into an even better college" or "My niece who is younger to you gets paid way more than that." They never really let you enjoy your achievements and never waste a minute to burst your bubble. We also have friends who would take pride in failing together, but if you pass and they fail, they sure treat you like a traitor. They are never ready to be responsible and be committed to the group study you planned but are sure to blame you if you pass and they don't. They fail to see their shortcoming. They belittle your achievements and you and never appreciate your growth. These kinds of people put out the fire in you, these are the kind of people you have to stay away from.

One of the major reason startups fail is not because of a bad idea or a bad decision. It's because the founders gave up too soon. They lose sight of why they started the business and when they face any problem, instead of finding a solution they give up. They lose energy from within. To make sure you don't lose your rhythm and stay positive you should hang around with likeminded people. Everybody will die one day; every business will die or evolve. Pick and choose the people you connect and network with. You are an ice cube, if you are with fire you will melt. Don't hang around with such negative people who say you are not good enough!

But also keep in mind, without proving your worth, you can't expect people around you to be supportive as well. If they don't see you as a responsible person who can win their trust, they are not going to be trusting and supportive of you. Also, the people around you are not only your friends and family but also include your co-founders, employees and other stakeholders in your business. If you manage to put together a focused and enthusiastic bunch of people to form your team, you are going to build better products for your customers and solve problems at ease. Instead, if your team lacks energy they might very well contribute to the failure of your start-up. So, when you are thinking of finding co-founders and employees to work under you, it's not the mere numbers you will have to focus on, it is the quality of the resource that matters. They have to believe in the idea the way you do. They have to share the same spirit to make your idea a reality and take it closer to prospective customers. Associating with the right people is one of the key aspects determining the success of your entrepreneurship journey.

Risky is the New Sexy

RITESH AGARWAL

VIJAY SHEKHAR SHARMA

KUNAL SHAH

Now that you have a fair idea of what are the kinds of resources you need, you got to evaluate your scenario as to where you currently stand and what is your risk appetite. Now, when I say risk, in the entrepreneurial context, it refers to the calculated risk and not a gamblers risk. Once you have accessed the availability of your resources and the level of risk you are willing to take you can evaluate where to begin your entrepreneurial journey. The below matrix would help you decide if you still have your doubts about what could be an ideal avenue for you guys to start at.

Resources	Risk: Low	Medium	High	Very High
Very High	Franchise	Business	Start Up	Start Up
High	Franchise	Business	Business	Start Up
Medium	Zero Investment	Franchise	Business	Business
Low	Zero Investment	Zero Investment	Franchise	Franchise

Zero Investment Options

These business ideas require the least resource spending and are a great place to start irrespective of where you have currently assessed yourself to be. If you are a beginner, you are more likely to make mistakes and sometimes mistakes can prove to be fatal. So, starting with zero investment options serves as a good ground to test yourself. Some of these ideas include social media influencing, YouTube videos, blogging, podcasting, drop shipping, freelance writing, virtual assistant, website flipping, online book publishing, SEO/SMO consulting, affiliate marketing, Facebook Ads consulting, Amazon associates, etc. There are loads of free content online for you to pick one of these skills and launch your first minimal investment venture.

Franchise Models

If you decide you can invest quite some resources into your venture but don't have enough experience running all aspects of a business, then becoming a franchisee could be the best fit for you. A good Franchise is usually a proven business model, a well-known trademark – which means finding customers is easier, the branding activities are centralized and above all, you would be handheld by a Franchisor who knows the nuances of the business. It gives you good exposure to run a real business, but at a lesser risk of failure!

Starting Your Own Business From Scratch

If you have adequate resources, experience and are willing to take more risk, you could move on to the next stage of starting your own venture. You are responsible for everything in the business and you have to own your failures and success stories. Right from building the product to finding the customers to getting paid for the offering, the only advantage you have is you have entered an existing domain and you have the benefit of learning from the mistakes of other players in the chosen field. Business is a tested and proven framework hence most of your work will be in executing the model.

The Startup

This is the most risk a person could take in their entrepreneurial journey. You have come up with an idea for a product or a service offering that doesn't exist at the moment and you believe you will be able to solve a certain problem or make life easier with your innovative solution. There is no proven market statistics that indicate that your idea is scalable. You on your own, paving your own path towards your goal. You are bound to face a lot of uncertainties and it requires a lot of passion and grit to make your startup idea a success. It is harder to find investors as there is no proven track record indicating the measure of success of your prospective venture. So, if your idea fits in as a solution to a persistent problem, then you can go ahead and startup!

So, let us access ourselves and start our entrepreneurship journey, shall we? As we grow and hone our entrepreneurial skills let's aim at moving higher up the spectrum and become the change-makers, we all want to be!

Predict or Perish

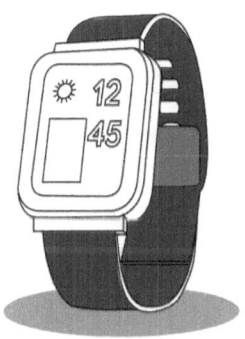

So, as an entrepreneur, you may either start a business or a startup. A business is where you are investing and building on a tried and tested approach whereas, in a startup you innovate. Both have their own perks. When it comes to a business you will face huge competition from existing businesses, there will be large scale manufacturers and service providers who have years of experience and benefits of large-scale operations and you are bound to suffer from rookie mistakes. But also, since it's a tried and tested approach, you are not blind sighted, and you have clarity on what could be your way forward and also people who might be willing to share their experience. But there is always a looming threat of becoming irrelevant and obsolete when a new invention makes it convenient, cheaper and faster. Like the touch screen models of Apple wiped out Nokia's dominance in the mobile phone industry you run the risk of becoming irrelevant when you don't think ahead of your time and innovate.

That's where a startup makes more sense. To predict the future, to innovate, to create a different approach, to add new features. While traditional watch manufacturers were only focused on the look, feel and shape of the watch, there were a bunch of technology geeks that thought of adding features like pedometers, heart rate trackers, calorie counters, message and call alerts and displays, music system controls, alarms and whatnot into that tiny wrist gadget that made so many people switch from suave grandpa watches to smartwatches. But not all ideas are a smartwatch or a smartphone idea. When you are rethinking the design and functionalities of a certain product or service you have to be prepared to put together everything it takes to make it a reality – manpower with the relevant technical expertise, manufacturers that can replicate your design needs, creating a demand for a never heard of product or service among the customers – to name a few.

When we started Kolapasi back in 2013, dine in restaurants were a huge deal. People were pouring in lakhs and crores to set up restaurants and there was a huge competition and also, a huge demand for a restaurant that could offer great ambience and delicious food. But we predicted that the next big wave would be takeaways/deliveries. Not only was it easily scalable, but it also cost us under Rs 10 lakhs to set up a takeaway or a cloud kitchen. Now we have set up multiple outlets in Tamil Nadu and are in the process of setting up outlets in Bangalore and even expanding internationally with discussions underway to establish outlets in Australia, Singapore and in the US! Cloud Kitchen though a common thing now, was an innovation and a new concept back in those days and that did pay off!

Even if you start a business, you would have to access your market and innovate on time. If you don't predict, you perish!

The rule to follow is that "You build your startup for the next curve and not for the existing curve"

Profit vs The Learning Curve

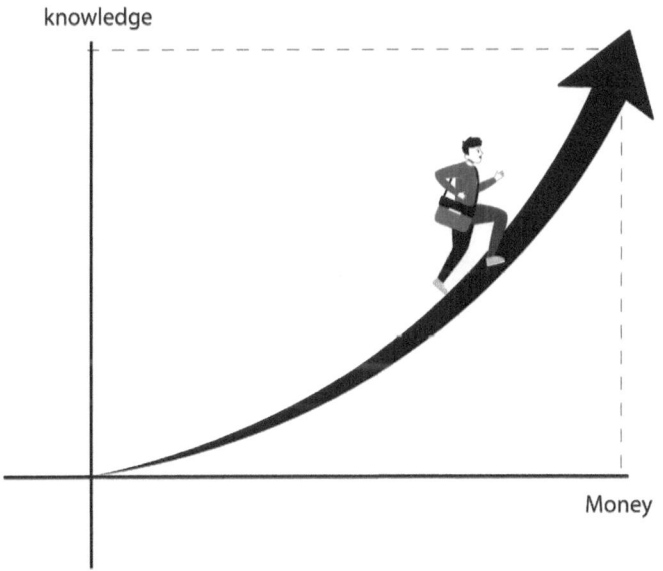

> *"90% of new startups fail. 75% of venture-backed startups fail. Under 50% of businesses make it to their fifth year. 33% of startups make it to the 10-year mark."*
>
> – As quoted from 2020 startup statistics by review42 reports

The above statement is the truth, the reality! But the one thing I don't agree with the above statement is the use of the term failure. Your success might not look like everybody else's, but what that entrepreneurial journey taught you, the lessons you learnt from your mistakes are for life and they will come in handy, no matter if you start another entrepreneurial venture or not.

In business either you make a profit, or you learn, you never make a loss.

Let's look at it this way. In your college, you pursued BE in Mechanical Engineering. But you got a job in a software company and are working as a computer engineer instead. Would you consider your college degree as a waste of time, money and energy? In school, until 10th grade, most of us had to study a whole lot of other subjects that are not relevant to what we do now. We might joke about how we never use all the complex algebra, trigonometry and calculus ever, but we don't write off our school education as an utter waste of time. It taught us some values, we made great friends, we had so many memorable experiences that all of us felt at least sad if not depressed at our farewells and were a tad bit too excited about our reunions.

Similarly, no matter what the outcome of your entrepreneurial efforts was, it's a journey with a huge learning curve. If you have heard any speech from an entrepreneur or read their biographies, they all have one thing in common – their valuable lessons learnt from their rookie mistakes. Just like a relationship that did not work out for you, a failed entrepreneurial journey can be like a breakup that teaches about what works for you and what does not and even makes you realize what's wrong with you, that you can change to become a better person.

If you want to do an MBA in India it would cost about Rs 5 lakhs to 30 Lakhs. If you want a fancier MBA from an Ivy League School, it would cost you about Rs 50 lakhs to Rs 1.5 crores. You spend one to two years making presentations on case studies, running surveys, doing summer internships. You would not call the money or the time you spent a waste rather call it an amazing experience that taught business etiquettes. Similarly, the entrepreneurial spirit that you gain, and the life lessons you learn is no match. Look at the bright side, pull up your socks and be ready to rewrite your story!

The Anticlimax

So far, I have tried setting your entrepreneurial thought process on a right track. And I can't insist enough about why it is important to become an entrepreneur for the right reasons and with the right mindset. There are a few common misconceptions and unrealistic expectations some of us have about becoming an entrepreneur. Those of you reading this book might be living in such a bubble too and by all means, I seek to burst it with this anticlimax. If you are planning to become an entrepreneur for the below reasons, with due respect and by all means, I would like to stop you from becoming one. Because if one becomes an entrepreneur for solely these reasons you are on a road to disappointment. So, let me be a devil's advocate and tell you why you should not become an entrepreneur for the following reasons.

Dropping Out of School/College Will Not Make You Bill Gates

You might have read articles or biographies of great minds like Steve Jobs, Elon Musk, Bill Gates, Mark Zuckerberg and so on who quit college to pursue their entrepreneurial journey. And it might make you think less of the current education system and daydream about quitting college and starting your entrepreneurial venture. But if you look into the lives of these guys, they were one of the smartest guys, studying in the most prestigious of the institutions and quit when they had this great idea and could not handle building their business and studying in a full-time college curriculum at the same time. Steve Jobs went to Reed College, Elon Musk was at Stanford, Bill Gates and Mark Zuckerberg were at Harvard. They had already proved their worth by finding their way into these global universities that are hard to get into in the first place. And all of them had an amazing idea that was consuming all their time leaving them with no time for a University education. It made more sense for them to quit than waste their time. In no way their decision to quit is the sole reason behind their success. They were smart, hardworking people who were a genius in their respective fields. They knew exactly what they were doing and had great vision and goals. So unless you have a great idea, have the smarts and grit it takes to build a business around that idea and there is absolutely no way you can manage your formal education and your growing business at the same time, do not quit. After all, finishing what one started is one of the key traits of a true entrepreneur!

Shortcut to Wealth and Fame

Entrepreneurship is the hardest way to find wealth and fame for exactly one reason – the risk it involves. If you play the game right it certainly might put you on a fast track route to a lifetime's worth of fortune. But it is a route that expects you to navigate many sharp turns overlooking a fatal fall into the valley below. And one wrong manoeuvre might cost you your life, in this case, the years, efforts, money and everything you have fed into your business. And you should know how to fix a flat tyre, an overheated engine, a leaky fuel tank, a not so functional brake system and ride on an unknown muddy, murky terrain through sunshine and storms. Take Steve Jobs for example. We all know he was thrown out of Apple, his own brainchild until he found his bearings and jumped back on the saddle. Also, not all entrepreneurs make it big. There are so many businesses that started small and remained small forever until it was wiped out of existence.

We have all heard about K Vaitheeswaran, who started India's first e-commerce website Fabmart. com back in 1999. He was ahead of his time and had close to a decade long head start as compared to today's successful e-commerce sites like Flipkart, despite which he couldn't make it in the Indian e-commerce space. But he proved to be a Phoenix, he got out of the rut and went on to pen down his journey and released the book "Failing to Succeed – the story of India's first e-commerce company" which is part of the Amazon collective – Memorable business books of 2017! He is widely hailed as the 'father of e-commerce in India'. In his own words in an interview with thenewsminute.com he described the nature of startups-

"There is a lot that's going on in the startup ecosystem. There is a lot of glamour associated with it. There are two sides to every coin. In this case, one side is the success and the glamour that comes with it and then there the other side where a large number of startups don't do well. They shut down because the financial outcome was not as planned. And that's because startups by nature are very high-risk high-reward. But there is the third side of the coin as well. When the coin stands on its side. This third side is the dark side that destroys people completely. And I had to go through it with my startup."

Be Your Own Boss

While you might be leading your company and people working under you, you are expected to step into the shoes of every role in the organization. You no more can just be focusing on your role, because your role as an entrepreneur is going to be super consuming. They say the consumer is the king for this very reason because you have to meet the consumer's needs and keep him convinced that your product or service is the best. Otherwise, you will run out of business. Running a business is like taking care of a baby, you need to feed it on time, with people and finance and you need to handhold it so much in the initial few years until you form a self-sufficient and experienced team to support various verticals of your business. And as it grows bigger, you are bound to face bigger, better and newer problems that you have to find solutions to. You won't have time to breathe.

Like Paul Graham, the founder of YCombinator, an American seed money startup accelerator, said, "If you start a startup it will take over your life to a degree that you cannot imagine. And if it succeeds it will take over your life for a long time for several years at the very least, maybe a decade, maybe the rest of your working life. So, there's a real opportunity cost here. It may seem to you that Larry Page has an enviable life, but there are parts of it that are definitely unenviable. The way the world looks to him is that he started running as fast as he could at the age of 25 and he has not stopped to catch his breath since. Every day, shit happens within the Google empire that only the emperor can deal with. And he, as the emperor has to deal with it. If he goes on vacation for even a week, a whole lot of problems occur and accumulates and he has to bear this uncomplainingly, because, number one, as the company's daddy he can never show his fear or weakness and number two, if you are a billionaire you get zero, actually less than zero sympathy about having a difficult life!"

So, it is critical that you understand what you're signing up for here if you are planning to embark on an exciting journey of becoming an entrepreneur. And once you are bitten by this bug, and you taste some success, there is no turning back!

Just Jump!

I quote this in every gathering I am invited to address.

"Thinking of becoming an entrepreneur is a torture but becoming one is easy."

A couple of years ago, I happened to comment on a post of a dear friend, Bhargavi, who did bungee jumping in Singapore – "This is awesome! Let's do it when I come to Singapore!", though I never had the intention of doing it ever. I find the idea of bungee jumping ridiculous. Who in their right mind will pay over Rs.20000, sign a waiver form that says "I won't sue if I happen to die or lose a limb", take the effort to climb up several hundred feet off the ground and jump off a cliff when nobody is holding them at gunpoint?

After two months or so I happened to visit Singapore and on day one I got a call from a super excited Bhargavi – Let's go bungee jumping! I never thought she would remember and hold me to act on a silly comment that I posted months ago! But I could not lose face saying I am afraid. I put on a fake macho attitude about it, though I could feel an intestine wrapping around my heart kind of twisting in my gut and she took me to AJ Hackett Sentosa and dragged me all the way up through 17 fleets of stairs. Once I was strapped in and the gear was double-checked, I was directed to the edge.

Standing at the edge of the leaping station, looking down at the 50 meters leap I had the biggest revelation in my life (my Newtonian moment). The longer I stood on the ledge, the higher the chances I wouldn't make the jump. My brain was giving me all logical reasons as to why I shouldn't make the jump like "Santhosh, you have family, you have a business to take care of and what if something happens to you?". All of these reasons were so logical that you could not ignore them. I realized that if I prolonged my jump by a few seconds, I wouldn't have taken the jump, so I closed my eyes and took the blind leap of faith. I am neither religious nor an atheist but I prayed to every god and soul up in heaven. I did not want to die that day. Though I was tied securely to a cord and a harness, there is a chance that I might die of a heart attack from the shock one's body goes through when they drop.

The experience, as frightening as it was, was also magical. Then the cord slowed my fall and the fear disappeared as I experienced a giant bounce as the cord stretched to its full length, breaking my free fall. I felt like I defied gravity and felt so weightless. And in no time, I was swinging like a pendulum, totally enjoying the full view of the Sentosa beach, feeling so Zen, slowing down to a standstill, nothing but the sound of the waves and the warm summer breeze. That moment was mine; I earned it.

Leaping that ledge was a huge thrill. But it was so much more! I felt like I was in control, face to face battling my fear, realizing that the fear was nothing after all. "Everything you've ever wanted is on the other side of fear", a famous quote by George Addair. Becoming an entrepreneur is not an exception to the rule. It is so much like bungee jumping. When you have decided to become an entrepreneur, you just got to do it. Take that leap of faith! In hindsight, this whole situation was similar to that of Newton's story with his apple, to me. With this experience, I came up with my fundamental law of life

"The longer you think of doing something, the higher are the chances that you will not do it."

We never decide to do anything right away! We never plan anything for our present. Hitting the gym, pursuing a hobby, everything has to be a new year's resolution. Our intentions are right, but we are always tricked by our brain into not taking action. It finds a way to make us feel good about deciding to take action in the future and keep us rooted in our autopilot habitual behaviour. There are so many psychological studies that prove this to be a fact. Most of you would have heard of Mel Robbins – "5-second rule". In a nutshell, the rule says it takes 5 seconds to take action on a thought or to let yourself be clouded by your fears and come up with a classic excuse for discarding that thought. All we have is a 5-second window since a thought arises, to follow it with action or inaction. Unless we realize this, we are a perpetual victim to the 5-second rule. To overcome this, she recommends counting backwards, 5, 4, 3, 2, 1 and spring into action. This counting in reverse is a starting ritual of sorts, to break our pattern of letting our brain come up with an excuse for not doing something and switching from inaction to action.

I have been taking the jumps since I moved from the USA, first one was to start a venture in Hyderabad for garments. I took another jump when I decided to start my second venture, Kolapasi. Life is all about taking the leap and stepping out of our comfort zone, we humans are a creature of habit, our brain is wired to protect ourselves. We have a sense of calm when we are doing our routine habits. We have to be prepared and equipped to jump and not keep thinking of what could possibly happen if we didn't try something. I wanted to take the leap into my business venture solely because I thought about it well but not too well-crafted to perfection. I took the jump and was prepared to do whatever it takes at Kolapasi; I followed the steps given in this book, got the spark and knew how to think to kickstart my business.

When I started realizing my own habitual procrastination of 'to do or not to do' something, I thought of my bungee jumping experience and I reminded myself the moment just before I jumped.

It was my switch from inaction to action! Find yours!

The Indian Edge

"2020 will produce the highest number of entrepreneurs ever. More problems to be solved, so more entrepreneurs will emerge!"

Today, India is pinned to be a wonderland for investments. India sports a huge market base and is witnessing an exponential increase in per capita spending, especially driven by the middle class. Currently, the Indian annual consumer spending is pegged at 21 trillion INR (for those of you who are wondering that's 12 zeros). According to an article published by the World Economic Forum, by 2030, Indian spending is projected to increase 4x times. Nearly 80% of households in 2030 will fall under the middle-income group, up from about 50% today. The middle class will drive 75% of consumer spending in 2030. The laws for foreign investments have been liberalized since 1995 and more so with every fiscal year.

The world's second-highest population, robust domestic demand, high purchasing power, economic liberalization and cheap labour attracts foreign investment in India. Cost competitiveness and an epic pool of talent make India one of the most preferred destinations for FDI. India is considered the most lucrative Asian Market because of its liberalized and democratic setup which promotes private businesses to flourish without a lot of regulatory red tapes.

Institutional investors around the world are pumping money into India by funding the startups that are focusing on capturing consumer demand such as Swiggy, Zomato, Flipkart, Ola, Bounce etc. These businesses are currently nowhere close to even breaking even. But why are they investing billions of dollars in these businesses? Because they want to tap into the Indian consumer base. They want to acquire the market with the greatest growth potential. What is that these foreign investors see that we are so oblivious to? What is the opportunity that we are missing on by letting these foreign investors garner a greater customer base in India than any homegrown Indian business? Let me elaborate on why India is such a crucial market that global investors are seizing every single opportunity to get some action here. The following data includes excerpts from various publishing of the World Economic Forum.

Shift In The Income Levels

In India, the households are clubbed into four broad buckets based on the per capita earnings of the household. On an average, less than Rs 70k per capita earnings is low-income group, Rs 70k to Rs 270k is the lower-middle-income group, Rs 270k to Rs 850k the upper-middle-income group and anything above Rs 850k the high-income group. Currently, India is categorized as a lower-middle-income country with 50% of the population in the lower-middle-income group. By 2030, India will move from being a lower-middle-income economy to one led by the middle class. Nearly 80% of households in 2030 will be middle-income and will drive 75% of consumer spending in 2030.

Increase In Income Mobility Will Drive Growth Across All Consumption Categories

As 140 million households move into the middle class and another 20 million move into the high-income bracket, they will spend 2-2.5x more on essential categories (food, beverages, apparel, personal care, gadgets, transport and housing) and 3-4x more on services (healthcare, education, entertainment and household care). Upper-middle-income and high-income entrants will drive a 15-20% increase in the ownership of durables (washing machines, refrigerators, TVs and personal vehicles). Also, half of the incremental purchasing power will go into buying the existing products and services being consumed now. However, the other half will be spent on upgrading to premium offerings and including new variants in existing routines, such as adding organic food items and a new skincare regime or adopting app-based ridesharing. Premiumization and category addition will drive a significant share of increased spending on eating (food and beverages at home, and dining out), looking good (personal care and apparel) and staying connected (cellphones, data packs and gadgets).

Benefits of Higher Penetration of Internet and Smartphones

The internet and smartphones have significantly bridged the information divide between consumers in urban and rural India. By 2030, more than 40% of all purchases will be highly digitally influenced, up from 20-22% today. Beyond the top 40 cities, developed rural and small urban towns already have a very similar income profile. At a given income level, both these consumer groups desire a similar standard of living, aspire to a similar set of brands and are equally comfortable with technology-enabled consumption. Rural India's strong desire to consume is presently constrained by poor access to roads, power, organized retail and financial services. Future efforts to improve physical and digital connectivity, and the use of innovative distribution channels, will enhance well-being and unlock the true consumption potential of rural India. Also, there will be a surge in the consumers willing to pay for online streaming services like those of Netflix and Amazon Prime, especially for entertainment and news.

Businesses That Bridge the Generation Gap Between Their Product/Service Offering and Millennial and Generation Z Preferences Will Significantly Shape The Market

Like there will be a shift in income levels of the household there will also be a shift in the generation of the consumer base from Boomers to Gen Y, Gen Z and Millennials. These consumers will be able and willing to spend more but will also be more discerning. In 2030, 77% of Indians will be born in the late 1980s and onwards. This generation of consumers will have had exposure to more product and service options than their predecessors. These youngest Indians already exhibit the greatest willingness to increase spending over the next 10 years, but they are also highly discerning about what they consider "best in class" offerings in every consumption category, from apparel to cars. Businesses will have richer, more willing buyers, but these buyers will be highly informed and make very specific choices for themselves and their families.

Also, unlike other generations, they will be more concerned about the social impact of their consumption. Businesses that place themselves as brands that care about fair trade, better economic and hygienic conditions for labour, the carbon footprint of their consumption, breeding conditions of animals, ethical fishing and agricultural practices, etc. will be preferred over other products and services. These will be the major distinguishing factors for the consumers from this generation.

India's Eternal Hunt for 'Value For Money' Brands

Indian consumers will be willing to adopt value-for-money brands that have "just right" features and prices. India's new consumers aspire to consume more (and the necessary income to fulfil this desire), but they are dispersed across tens of thousands of urban and rural towns. Asset-light e-commerce models, supported by offline partnerships and demand-aggregators, will help brands test out and reach these new markets in a cost-efficient manner. Businesses will also have an opportunity to unlock spend on new category extensions.

For instance, dining out will become a significant area of food and beverage spend (up from more than 10% today), driven by the increasing use of app-based meal deliveries to replace home-cooked meals, especially by upper-middle-income and high-income working consumers. One in four of these consumers has already begun to increase their spend on entertainment to subscribe to digital video-streaming services. Affordable and innovative options can unlock massive incremental spend and establish new variants of consumption in many existing categories.

Technology-Enabled New Business Models Will Leverage Inherent Comfort With 'Usership' and The Desire For Increased Convenience and Well-Being

As the original usership economy, India has lessons for the world. Indians have traditionally preferred using public transport services over owning vehicles, and furnished homes using low-cost second-hand furniture rather than new purchases. Digital platforms for renting and sharing will speak to this usership mindset, as well as to the tech-savviness of future consumers. Subscription models, much like today's Bombay Shaving Club, Amazon India Grocery Pantry and Fab Bag, will serve the value-conscious Indian keen to access new brands and products for a small recurring spend. Digital platforms for health and learning will fulfil the Indian consumer's prime aspiration – the desire for greater well-being for themselves and their family.

There Will Be an Increasing Demand for Social Impact Startups

India presents a host of exciting business opportunities in the next decade. At the same time, the next phase of India's growth story offers stakeholders a chance to shape a path of responsible and equitable growth, from which other fast-growing markets can learn. Building on the momentum of collaborative efforts such as Skill India and Eat Right India, public-private-civil-society partnerships can help tackle the three key societal challenges facing India today: the need for skills and jobs for its working-age majority; the greater inclusion of rural India; and the building of a healthy and sustainable future for its citizens and cities. As the millennials and Generation-Z take over as the earning adults of the country there will be a boom in Ethical Consumerism and there will be a huge shift in consumer loyalty.

By now I am pretty sure I have sold to you on why India is a great place to start your business. While there are foreign investors who are willing to build firms that will thrive by innovating for India and embracing a 'founder's mentality' we have to realize our own potential and start embracing the latest digital technology that is highly shaping the consumption pattern in India. We have to leverage the opportunity at hand and upskill to upscale. Factors such as convenience, value for money, social impact and ethical consumerism have already started creating a drift in the Indian markets. It doesn't matter if you have years of experience doing business or if you are a newbie. Unless you understand the nuances of the dynamic Indian consumer you will not survive this new wave that is picking momentum. And no one can know an Indian consumer better than an Indian consumer himself, yes, you! KFC, McDonalds, Dominos, Pizza hut and all other multinational restaurant chains had customized their pizzas, burgers and pasta to appeal to the Indian palette. If you have gone abroad and tasted the authentic food in the origin country, you would agree with me that to like these foods in their original, authentic form for an uninitiated Indian would be next to impossible. It's an acquired taste and never can be the food of the masses in India like they are right now. That is why I insist you have to find your paneer for your pizza. If you want to crack the Indian customer code, you have to think like an Indian customer. And who can do the job better than an Indian customer?

Cardinal Rules

"If you are looking for inspiration to start your startup, then don't start one!"

1. Uncertainty is the only certainty and change is the only constant. Brace yourself to face the surprises and challenges to level up and keep playing the game.
2. Know your why? Become an entrepreneur only if you have the spirit for building a product or service for your customers. Not because of the fame and money it offers.
3. Don't rebel when you don't have to. Pick your battles. Choose peace and harmony over being a rebel. Get your people on board. Don't make everything a "world versus you" scenario when it is not. Build your reputation instead.
4. There are 3 key elements every entrepreneur needs – Money, knowledge and emotional bandwidth to enjoy the roller-coaster ride of starting up and running a business.
5. Don't look down upon employment. Employment and entrepreneurship are two sides of the same coin. Do your job with an entrepreneurial spirit, gain some hands-on experience and you are sure to become a better entrepreneur.
6. Connect and associate with like-minded people. You will burn out if you don't have a

support system that holds you up through the journey.

7. If you are afraid of taking risks, entrepreneurship is not for you. Times like the COVID19 global pandemic would have shown you that even employment is not a safe bet. Risk and uncertainty are part and parcel of everyone's life!

8. The ability to predict and innovate is a mark of a great entrepreneur. Focus on staying ahead of the curve and offering an enhanced experience to your customers. If you don't innovate then you become obsolete!

9. Be prepared to make mistakes and learn from them. Embrace the learning curve.

10. The best time to start your business is yesterday, you are already running late! Take that leap of faith and become an entrepreneur instead of feeding your doubts and fears! Just Jump!

11. Don't seek motivation from the outside world. It won't last. It is the fire from within that will help you reach your destiny.

www.ingramcontent.com/pod-product-compliance
Lightning Source LLC
Chambersburg PA
CBHW030906180526
45163CB00004B/1729